T0199166

The Day Walt Met Me

Aleesa St. Julian

The Day Walt Met Me

This book is dedicated to
the Memory of Walt Baby Love.

In honor of the love of our community, partial proceeds from this book will be donated to First Priority of North Alabama.

I might be little, but I serve a

BIG GOD!

Something Aleesa wants you to know...

GOD blessed Aleesa with an ability to read when she was a baby.

But...

She still learned that life isn't a piece of cake. She wishes it was because she loves cake. Life has happy moments but difficult ones too. Sometimes sad things happen that are out of our control. However, GOD can even make tough times easier. We shouldn't give up on GOD because HE will never give up on us.

So many people in the world are sad and need to know that JESUS can help them. GOD gave you special talents and gifts that can help you in life and can be used to help others know more about JESUS. GOD used Aleesa's ability of reading and writing to allow her to write Christian books. She published her first book at the age of six. It's called, *The Day I Met Walt.* GOD showed her how to use her gift for good things instead of bad things.

However, sometimes when you're trying to use your gifts the right way, people may make fun of you or talk about you. But forgive them, and don't let that stop you because GOD is still on your side and will help you and bless you! You see, people make mistakes.

It's so good to have a loving church family, but sometimes even people who go to church may mistreat others. If someone is ever mean to you, remember that GOD still loves you and wants you to talk with HIM about your struggles. HE may also lead you to find someone you can trust to help you.

Aleesa and her family have been blessed to have a loving church family and community! There's also a church family right for you, and GOD can help you find them! Even then, everyone there may not do everything perfectly, but you will be able to tell when the majority of people around you truly love you and others.

Always remember that GOD wants to help us get through life's difficulties. Tough times can even make us stronger if we ask GOD to help us. Choose to do good over bad because you never know how your right decisions might help others stop making bad ones.

Let's enjoy our godly lives and help others find joy in theirs too!

Then JESUS came to them and said, "All authority in heaven and on earth has been given to me. Therefore go and make disciples of all nations, baptizing them in the name of the Father and of the Son and of the Holy Spirit, and teaching them to obey everything I have commanded you. And surely I am with you always, to the very end of the age" Matthew 28:18-20.

The Day Walt Met Me

Once upon a time, there was a little boy named Walt. His mom wanted him to sing in her church, but he was shy and didn't want to do it.

Yet, when he became a man, he realized GOD gave him the gift of singing; so, he finally started singing in a church. One day bullies asked him not to sing there anymore. Walt sadly stopped going to church.

Now, I am going to tell you a little bit about me. I'm the author of this book, and my name is Aleesa. When I was younger, I was afraid of the dark. I asked my momma to pray for me.

One night when I was scared, GOD led my momma to sing a song called, "Amazing Grace." I cried (happy tears) and said, "Momma, when you sing that song, I'm not afraid anymore." That night, GOD took away my fears of the dark!

Weeks later, it was *The Day I Met Walt.* Our church family decided to take food to people who needed help in our community. A man named, Walt, saw me. He walked over and started singing, "Amazing Grace!" He also gave me a stuffy! It made me so happy to hear him singing the same song that Momma sang to me at night! Afterwards, I told him how much that song meant to me and how GOD used that song to take away my fears of the dark.

The Day Walt Met Me, he realized GOD wanted him to keep singing and that GOD was going to really bless people through his gift of singing. GOD touched Walt's heart; so, Walt began the process of forgiving those people who told him not to sing in that church.

Walt began going to my church and became part of my family. So, on Walt's 70th Birthday, we were on our way to visit him. We bought his favorite double chocolate cake covered in chocolate icing. Mmmmmmm...

But on our way, we received the saddest phone call. Walt passed away. I cried, but GOD had already planned a way for me to feel better. I didn't know this at the time, but right before Walt passed away, he received a DVD from people in his old church. He gave it to Momma. Since I was so sad that Walt was gone, Momma decided to play the DVD.

I was amazed to see what GOD did for us! It was a video of Walt singing, "Amazing Grace" in a church! God planned a way for me to feel better and to still be able to hear Walt singing my favorite song! I knew that Walt was happy singing in Heaven and probably eating the type of cake that would knock your socks off!

I also knew there were a few things Walt would want me to do, and the first thing was to share his double chocolate cake covered in chocolate icing with my big brother, Avery.

Walt couldn't be the only one eating cake!

The second thing Walt would want me to do is to remind all of you to use your gifts and talents to glorify GOD because the world needs to know that Jesus loves all of us soooooooooo much!

Thirdly,

I believe Walt would also want me to let you know about this verse from JESUS…

[JESUS states] "…In this world you will have trouble. But take heart! I have overcome the world."

(part of John 16:33)

Scriptures taken from the Holy Bible, New International Version®, NIV®. Copyright © 1973,
1978, 1984, 2011 by Biblica, Inc.™ Used by permission of Zondervan. All rights reserved
worldwide. www.zondervan.com The "NIV" and "New International Version" are trademarks
registered in the United States Patent and Trademark Office by Biblica, Inc.™

This book is a work of non-fiction. Unless otherwise noted, the author and the publisher make
no explicit guarantees as to the accuracy of the information contained in this book and in
some cases, names of people and places have been altered to protect their privacy.

WestBow Press books may be ordered through booksellers or by contacting:

WestBow Press
A Division of Thomas Nelson & Zondervan
1663 Liberty Drive
Bloomington, IN 47403
www.westbowpress.com
1 (866) 928-1240

Because of the dynamic nature of the Internet, any web addresses or links contained
in this book may have changed since publication and may no longer be valid. The views
expressed in this work are solely those of the author and do not necessarily reflect the views
of the publisher, and the publisher hereby disclaims any responsibility for them.

Any people depicted in stock imagery provided by Getty Images are models,
and such images are being used for illustrative purposes only.
Certain stock imagery © Getty Images.

ISBN: 978-1-9736-5987-7 (sc)
ISBN: 978-1-9736-5988-4 (e)

Library of Congress Control Number: 2019904389

Print information available on the last page.

WestBow Press rev. date: 4/16/2019

WestBow
PRESS®
A DIVISION OF THOMAS NELSON
& ZONDERVAN

Printed in the United States
By Bookmasters